P9-DMT-427

MAGIC WORDS

POEMS BY EDWARD FIELD

Based on songs and stories of the Netsilik Inuit, collected by Knud Rasmussen

Illustrated by Stefano Vitale

Gulliver Books
Harcourt Brace & Company
SAN DIEGO   NEW YORK   LONDON

Gulliver Books is a registered trademark of Harcourt Brace & Company.

The poems in this book first appeared in *Man: A Course of Study*,
a social science curriculum developed by Education Development
Center, Inc., under a grant from the National Science Foundation.

Library of Congress Cataloging-in-Publication Data
Field, Edward, 1924–
Magic words/poems by Edward Field; based on
songs and stories of the Netsilik Inuit collected by
Knud Rasmussen; illustrated by Stefano Vitale.
p. cm.
"Gulliver Books."
Summary: A collection of poems based on songs and stories
gathered by Knud Rasmussen on the Fifth Thule Expedition,
which recorded Inuit legends about the universe and its creation.
ISBN 0-15-201498-5
1. Inuit—Folklore—Juvenile poetry. 2. Cosmology—Juvenile poetry.
3. Inuit—Religion—Juvenile poetry. 4. Children's poetry, American.
[1. Inuit—Folklore—Poetry. 2. Eskimos—Folklore—Poetry.
3. Folklore—Arctic regions—Poetry. 4. Creation—Poetry.
5. American poetry.] I. Rasmussen, Knud, 1879–1933
II. Vitale, Stefano, ill. III. Title
PS3556.I37M34 1998
811'.54—dc20   96–20465

First edition
A C E F D B

PRINTED IN HONG KONG

The illustrations in this book were
done in oil paints on bark, wood, and stones.
Photography by Ted Morrison, New York, New York
The text type was set in Trump Mediaeval.
The display type was set in Albertus.
Color separations by Bright Arts, Ltd., Hong Kong
Printed by South China Printing Company, Ltd., Hong Kong
This book was printed on totally chlorine-free Nymolla Matte Art paper.
Production supervision by Ginger Boyer and Stanley Redfern
Designed by Michael Farmer

For Elsa Dorfman, photographer,
who connected me to the Inuit
—E. F.

To the Inuit people, and to all other
native people of North America
—S. V.

A NOTE ABOUT THE POEMS

THIS COLLECTION OF POEMS came to be thanks to a remarkable Dane named Knud Rasmussen, who spent his life among the people often called Eskimos but who call themselves Inuit.

Rasmussen was born in 1879 in Greenland, which was then a Danish possession. Except for the southern tip, Greenland's landscape is rugged, sculpted with ice mountains and fissured glaciers. Knud's father was from Denmark and worked as a missionary in an isolated Inuit settlement on the coast. Knud's mother, born in Greenland, was in fact part Inuit. Growing up with Inuit children, Knud learned Inuit as his second language, after Danish.

Knud was sent "home" to Denmark for his education, but in 1902, when he was twenty-three, he returned to Greenland and began exploring its upper reaches. He devoted most of the rest of his life to tracking his mother's, and his own, Inuit heritage across the Arctic Circle, where many Inuit communities were still living in their traditional way. With his knowledge of the Inuit language, Rasmussen naturally became a bridge between the Inuit and the rest of the world. His books about his travels and the people he met became best-sellers, and the photo of his ruggedly handsome face under the hood of a fur parka, his eyebrows iced, was recognized by millions around the world.

In 1921 Knud set off on what would become his most famous voyage, the Fifth Thule Expedition (*thule* being the Greek word for the "far north"), to try to settle the question of where the Inuit people had come from. Starting from his base in Greenland, Knud traveled by dogsled across eighteen hundred miles of the northern limits of the American continent above the Arctic Circle. It took him three years to get to Alaska, and in this land of no trees, which was ice- and snowbound for most of the year, Knud survived just as the Inuit themselves did. He spent many months with Inuit tribes, sharing their lives and writing in his journals everything the people told him about their world.

The Inuit had no written language, but they had a literary tradition and composed poems and songs quite consciously—magic songs to help in hunting caribou, seal, and polar bear; songs taunting their rivals in hunting and fishing; songs of the loneliness of old age or of long treks across the snowy landscape. One well-known poet named Orpingalik explained to Rasmussen, in words that many a modern poet would agree with, that "songs are thoughts, sung out on the breath, when people are moved by great feelings, and ordinary speech is no longer enough."

The "great feelings," feelings of awe and wonder, are evident in the four fascinating volumes of Knud's journals that were eventually published by the Royal Danish Archives. These journals are a treasure trove of Inuit lore. I drew on this material to create this selection of their legends, which deals with what the Inuit told Rasmussen about the universe and its creation: the sky, the stars, the weather, and the creatures with whom they share their land of snow and ice. Inspired by both the songs the poets sang for Rasmussen and the stories and legends ordinary people told him, I have tried to recapture Inuit voices in poems in our own language. I hope that the reader can imagine real people speaking—in this case the Inuit, in all their history and humanity.

—EDWARD FIELD

THE EARTH AND THE PEOPLE

The earth was here before the people.
The very first people
came out of the ground.
Everything came from the ground,
even caribou.
Children once grew
out of the ground
just as flowers do.
Women out wandering
found them sprawling on the grass
and took them home and nursed them.
That way people multiplied.

This land of ours
has become habitable
because we came here
and learned to hunt.
Even so, up here where we live
life is one continuous fight
for food and clothing
and a struggle against bad hunting
and snowstorms and sickness.

But we know our land is not the whole world.

MAGIC WORDS

In the very earliest time,
when both people and animals lived on earth,
a person could become an animal if he wanted to
and an animal could become a human being.
Sometimes they were people
and sometimes animals,
and there was no difference.
All spoke the same language.

That was the time when words were like magic.
The human mind had mysterious powers.
A word spoken by chance
might have strange consequences.
It would suddenly come alive
and what people wanted to happen could happen.
All you had to do was say it.
Nobody could explain this,
that's just the way it was.

DAY AND NIGHT:

HOW THEY CAME TO BE

In those times
when just saying a word
could make something happen,
there was no light on earth yet.
Everything was in darkness all the time,
people lived in darkness.

A fox and a hare had an argument,
each saying his magic word:
"Darkness," said the fox,
for he wanted it to be dark so he could go hunting.

"Day," said the hare,
for he wanted daylight
so he could find good grass to eat.

The hare won—his word was more powerful
and he got his wish:
Day came, replacing night.
But the word of the fox was powerful, too,
and when day was over, night came,
and from then on they took turns with each other,
the nighttime of the fox
following the daytime of the hare.

THUNDER AND LIGHTNING

Once in a time of hunger
the people were on the move
looking for better hunting grounds.
Coming to a wide rushing river,
the men made a ferry out of the kayaks
by tying them together with thongs
and brought the women and children across.

There were two orphans
whom nobody would bother about:
In the hungry times people only had enough
for their own children.
So no one took them
and they were left behind on the shore.

They stood there, the little boy and little girl,
watching the people go off without them.
How would they live? They had nothing to eat
and did not know how to take care of themselves.

They wandered back to the old campsite
to look for something to eat.
The girl only found a piece of flint,
and the boy, an old leather boot sole.

The boy said to his sister,
"After the way we have been treated,
I can't bear to be a human being any longer.
What can we turn into?"
"Caribou?" his sister suggested,
thinking of the warm herds and the moss to eat.
"No," he answered, "for then men would spear us to death."
"Seals?" she asked.
"No, for then they would tear us to pieces for food."

And in this way they named all the creatures,
but there wasn't one
that wasn't a victim of people.
Finally the sister proposed turning into thunder and lightning.
"That's it!" said her brother,
and they became airy spirits and rose into the sky,
the girl striking sparks with her flint
and the boy banging his piece of leather like a drum,
making the heavens flash and thunder.

They soon revenged themselves
 on the people who left them to starve.
   They made so much thunder and lightning over the camp
      that everyone died of fright.
         And that way people discovered
            that thunder and lightning could be
               very dangerous indeed.

THE THINGS IN THE SKY

The weather with its storms and snows
was once an orphan child
who was so cruelly treated, as orphans often are,
that he went up into the sky to take revenge.
That's where the bad weather came from
that ruins hunting and brings hunger.

The stars, too, are people
who suddenly raised themselves from the earth
and were fixed in the sky.
Some hunters were out chasing a bear
when they all rose up in the air
and became a group of stars.
Every constellation has such a story.

The northern lights are a celestial ball game:
They flicker over the sky
like a ball being kicked around
by players running on a field.

The rainbow is the shape of a great doorway,
opening, perhaps, to some world we still do not know.
But it is so far away
that no one has to be afraid
of the lovely colored light in the sky.

SUN AND MOON

A brother and sister had been very wicked.
They were so ashamed of themselves
they decided to change into something else
and start over in a new life.

The sister cried out of her unhappiness,
"Brother, what shall we turn into? Wolves?"

Her brother, not as anxious as she was to change, replied,
"Not wolves, sister, their teeth are so sharp."

"Brother, shall we be bears?" she asked desperately.
"Not bears, sister, they are too clumsy," he answered,
hoping she would accept his excuse.

"Brother, what in the world shall we be? Musk oxen?"
"Not musk oxen, their horns are too sharp."

"Brother, shall we be seals then?"
"No, sister, they have sharp claws."

And in this way they discussed all the animals,
but the brother didn't agree to any of them.

At last his sister moaned, "Brother,
shall we become the Sun and the Moon?"

Her brother really could think of no objection to that,
hard as he tried,
so they each lit a torch of moss from the fire
and holding the flames high,
they ran out of their snow hut.

They ran round and round it,
the brother chasing his sister faster and faster,
until they took off into the air.
They rose and rose and kept rising
right up into the sky.
But as they went, the sister put out her brother's torch
because he had been reluctant.

She with her lit torch became the Sun
and now warms the whole earth,
but her brother, the Moon, is cold
because his torch no longer burns.

HOW WE KNOW ABOUT ANIMALS

There was once a wise man
who turned himself into all the different kinds of animals
to see what it was like to be them.

That happened long ago in the old times
when there was not much difference yet
between an animal's soul and a human's,
so to change from one creature into another
was not too hard, if you knew how.
And this man knew the trick.

First he tried being a bear,
but that was a tiring life, they walk about so much.
Even at night they keep roaming, the furry wanderers.

When he had enough of that, he became a seal:
They are always playing in the water
making the waves go to and fro.
Seals like sports
and turn themselves into people sometimes for fun
and shoot at targets of snow, like we do,
with bows and arrows.

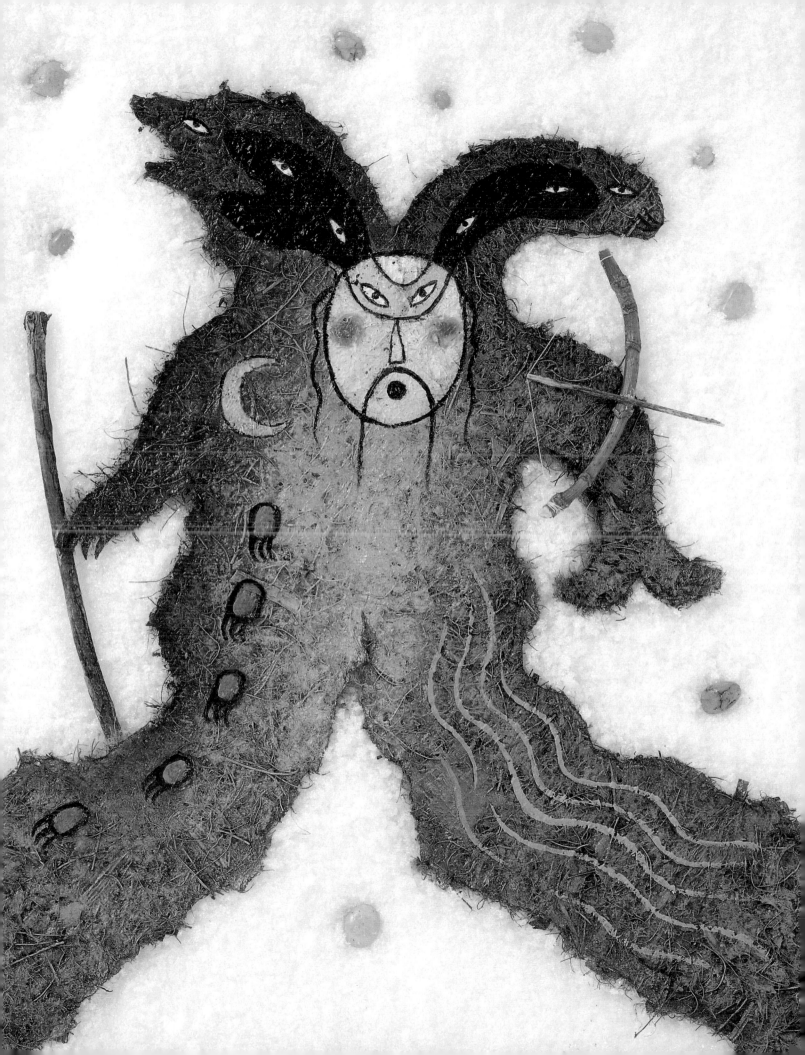

Then the wise man turned into a wolf,
but that was a hard life and he nearly starved
until another wolf showed him
how to get a good grip on the ground with his claws
and run with the pack.
That way he learned how to keep up with the others
and bring down caribou.

Then he became a musk ox:
How warm it was in the middle of the big lowing herds
huddled together.

And after that he became a caribou.
But caribou are strange beasts,
so timid that out of a sound sleep
they would jump up and gallop away
scared by a nothing.
How unpleasant to be a caribou!

That is how the wise man
lived the lives of all the animals.
He learned their secrets
and taught us all we know about them.

THE GIANT BEAR

There once was a giant bear
who followed people for his prey.
He was so big he swallowed them whole:
Then they smothered to death inside him
if they hadn't already died of fright.

Either the bear attacked them on the run,
or if they crawled into a cave,
where he could not squeeze his enormous body in,
he stabbed them with his whiskers like toothpicks,
drawing them out one by one,
and gulped them down.

No one knew what to do
until a wise man went out and let the bear swallow him,
sliding right down his throat into the big, dark, hot, slimy stomach.
And once inside the bear, he took a knife
and simply cut him open,
killing him of course.

He carved a door in the bear's belly
and threw out those who had been eaten before.
Then he stepped out himself
and went home to get help with the butchering.

Everyone lived on bear meat for a long time.
That's the way it goes:
Monster one minute, food the next.

HEAVEN AND HELL

And when we die at last,
we really know very little about what happens then.
But people who dream
have often seen the dead appear to them
just as they were in life.
Therefore we believe life does not end here on earth.

We have heard of three places where people go after death:
There is the Land of the Sky, a good place
where there is no sorrow and fear.
There have been wise men who went there
and came back to tell us about it:
They saw people playing ball, happy people
who did nothing but laugh and amuse themselves.
What we see from down here in the form of stars
are the lit windows of the villages of the dead
in the Land of the Sky.

Then there are two other worlds of the dead underground:
Way down deep is a place just like here on earth,
except on earth we starve
and down there they live in plenty.
The caribou graze in great herds,
and there are endless plains
with juicy berries that are nice to eat.
Down there, too, everything
is happiness and fun for the dead.

But there is another place, the Land of the Miserable,
right under the surface of the earth we walk on.
There go all the lazy men who were poor hunters,
and all the women who refused to be tattooed,
not caring to suffer a little to become beautiful.
They had no life in them when they lived,
so now after death they must squat on their haunches
with hanging heads, bad tempered and silent,
and live in hunger and idleness
because they wasted their lives.
Only when a butterfly comes flying by
do they lift their heads
(as young birds open pink mouths uselessly after a gnat),
and when they snap at it, a puff of dust
comes out of their dry throats.

Of course it may be
that all I have been telling you is wrong,
for you cannot be
certain about what you cannot see.
But these are the stories that our people tell.